Copyright ©2020 THEO WILLIAMS MD

All rights reserved. No part of this publication may be reproduced, distributed, or transmitted in any form or by any means, including photocopying, recording, or other electronic or mechanical methods, without the prior written permission of the publisher, except in the case of brief quotations embodied in critical reviews and certain other noncommercial uses permitted by copyright law.

Contents

Introduction

Landscape Architects and others in the field of landscape design often use the terms "softscape" and "hardscape" to distinguish between plants (soft) and rock or soil work and all the other "hard" elements of landscaping. A simple definition of "hardscape" is anything in the landscape that is not plantings, soils, or earth works.

At first thought, it might seem counterintuitive to think of 'hard'scaping as a wanted element in an environment designers often take great pains to keep natural and soft. So, why would this seemingly contradictory intrusion into the world of soft and floral be a critical part of any landscape design?

Hardscaping provides many added benefits beyond what plant and soil materials can accomplish on their own. Here are just a few of those reasons: Hardscaping areas provide contrast and added visual interest to planted spaces

They provide designated areas for user activities within the garden spaces, such as reading, gathering, eating, or relaxing

Hardscape elements are the most efficient materials to use to create accessibility within your natural spaces. Paths made of stone, brick, or compacted gravel provide a better walking or running surface than those made of organic materials such as hardwood mulch

Since hardscape materials are natural but inorganic they generally require much less long term maintenance and resources such as fertilizer and water.

What is Hardscape?

Hard scape consist of non living elements of landscaping, such as brick patio, a stone wall, or a wooden arbor. It is one of the two sub categories of landscaping, the other is soft scape.

Hardscaping can include almost any type of decorative or practical structure in a landscape, from driveways to fences to benches. Hardscape is a critical part of landscape design, providing definition and a sense of organization to the natural areas and features.

Hardscape elements can also define the use of a space, such as with a driveway, or it can lead visitors through different zones of softscaping, as with a gravel path that winds through a grassy area and into a secluded garden. There are so many ways to use hardscape elements to enhance your property:

- Stone retaining walls create planting areas or convert a slope to flat yard space.
- Concrete patios are the classic low-maintenance and versatile patio option.
- Brick patios offer a more upscale and natural look than concrete.
- Flagstone patios are the low-cost option for natural stone outdoor flooring.
- Tile patios are a great way to dress up a concrete patio slab.
- Stone walkways are ideal for garden paths.
- Gravel paths have a "softer" alternative to brick, concrete, or solid stone.
- Stone landscape steps have heavy stone slabs that make beautiful outdoor steps.
- Metal fences include coated steel, which is the modern standard, but iron is still an option.
- Wooden fences use the most versatile fence (and hardscaping) material—wood.
- Wooden decks are hardscaping, too, just like patios.

- Wooden arbors or gazebos enhance a landscape while providing shade.
- Pergolas are arbor-like structures attached to the house or other building.

How to use Rocks & other Hardscape Elements in your Garden Design

Hardscaping can be thought of as the bones, or framework, of a garden. It could be sleek flagstone patios, pebble mosaics, brick or rustic gravel walkways; perhaps a uniquely shaped boulder placed as a focal point in the garden or near a building to highlight architectural features. Natural stone, retaining walls, benches, seats, and sculptural landscape features, create the immovable structure through which designers (or handy diy homeowners) can easily weave in combinations of trees, plants, and shrubs into the garden tapestry.

Just as any good landscape designer should draw plant choices from the natural surrounding landscape, hardscape selection should also relate to the native environment as well as the style of house. For example, a colonial or Georgian house would benefit from the addition of brick or cut stone to add formality. A farmhouse in the countryside would combine well with fieldstone walls and paths of flagstone or flat river stones set in gravel. A Craftsman-style house in the city might call for a pattern of square and rectangular stones, and walls of cut or ashlar stone, or brick.

Archeticulally speaking, a good hardscape plan can help you divide the landscape into a collection of "rooms" or sequence of gardens. This is a timeless method of design as it provides separate spaces for different activities and a sense of surprise and thrill of discovery in moving from 'room to room'. Stone walls and hedges act as room dividers, and steps and paths act as transitions between these rooms, as well as the necessary means of moving between them.

 How a patio or terrace will be used in part should dictate your choice of paving material. Flat stones with mortared joints or sand-set brick are preferable for areas to close into the house, entries, and higher traffic areas. Irregular, dry-laid stones, crushed rock or packed decomposed granite are great for garden paths and casual areas. Dining areas or a seating terrace can be on stone, gravel or crushed rock, or wooden decking, depending in part on the furniture chosen for that use.

Factors to Consider When Choosing Hardscape Elements

- Color

Besides needing to harmonious with the colors found in the landscape plantings and architectural features, the color of your hardscape elements can play an important role. Light colored stone may help to brighten a shady corner but could also create glare in a sunnier spot. Dark stone materials might absorb too much heat for nearby planting materials.

- Porosity

The level of permeability a material has may matter more in some locations than others. A lava rock boulder, with its open honeycomb-like surface, would collect every fallen leaf and flower blossom if it were placed below a flowering ornamental tree. This might not be a bad thing, depending on what aesthetic you are going for or what level of garden maintenance you are willing to put into your landscape.

- Finish

Much like the porosity of stone materials, the finish can greatly affect the look, feel, and functionality of an outdoor area. Rough cut or chopped limestone blocks offer a rustic, natural feel while the same stone with a saw cut finished edge can transform a wall face or column top to a modern, sleek reveal. Additionally, when dealing with patio or walkway hardscape choices, consider how slick the stone finish will become during periods of precipitation or with a layer of snow or ice.

More factors to consider:

Paths need to be stable, easy to walk on, and preferably look like they belong. Again, a sense of fitting in with the natural landscape is important. Gravel, crushed rock and decomposed granite paths should ideally be edged, either with metal edging, wood timbers, or smaller brick or stone pieces. Dry-set paths of flagstone should use thicker stones 2" – 6". Stone steps need to be set in concrete for stability, unless they are fairly massive (5-6" thick).

The use of large, natural stones or boulders as pure design elements in the garden can help lift an ordinary planting plant to a new level of visual interest. Enormous granite boulders flecked with sparkly quartz, limestone or sandstone outcroppings that mimic those found in nature, large half-buried mossy fieldstones, or even a special grouping of uniquely shaped beach stones you found on your last vacation can help add a truly one of a kind feel to your landscape and make them "pop" with unusual interest.

So, if you're designing a new garden, or looking to rehabilitate a portion of one already in existence, think of the hardscape components just as carefully as you consider what trees, shrubs, and plants you want to put where. In the end, you'll have a more integrated, harmonious design, less maintenance, and a more interesting garden.

Hardscape Design

Hardscape is the "hard" features in your landscape. It is the heavier, unchanging, inanimate objects comprised of gravel, paving, stone and wood. Hardscape elements include:

- Walkways

- Patios

- Driveways

- Retaining Walls

- Swimming Pools

- Water Features

- Arbors

- Stone Benches

- Sprinkler Systems

Water Features as Hardscape

It may be somewhat counterintuitive, but even water features used in your yard count as hardscape. These structures assume a variety of forms, both with and without fountains:

- Stone fountains

- Ceramic fountains

- Inexpensive DIY fountains

- Clay pot fountains

With small water features containing a pool, the pool portion is often made with a preformed rigid plastic liner. With larger features, a nice alternative is a flexible rubber liner that allows you to make pools or ponds of almost any size or shape

Note:

Growing plants in and around a water feature is a great way to integrate hardscape and softscape within the same design.

How To Build Stone Retaining Walls Illustration

- Codes and Regulations

Check with your city's building authority for applicable building code rules and zoning laws governing retaining walls. Most areas require an engineer's stamp for walls over 3 feet, but some draw the line at 30 inches. Also, your city may require a permit and inspections for retaining walls of any height, even if you do the work yourself. Be sure to check before you build.

Warning :

Call before you dig. Before breaking ground on your project, call 8-1-1, the national "Call Before You Dig" hotline, to have all underground utility lines marked on your property. This is a free service that can take a few days, so call well in advance of starting your project.

What You'll Need:

Equipment / Tools

- Wood stakes
- Maul or hammer
- Mason's line
- Line level
- Shovel
- Wheelbarrow
- Utility knife
- Rake
- Short 2x4 board
- Hand tamp
- 4-foot carpenter's level
- Materials
- Field stone or cut stone
- Landscape fabric
- Compactible gravel
- Coarse sand
- Drainage gravel
- Masonry adhesive (optional)

Instructions:

- Organize the Stones

Organize the wall stones roughly by size and shape, making different piles as needed. You will use the largest, flattest stones for the base of the wall, and reserve the widest, smoothest, and best-looking stones for the capstones at the top of the wall. Keep in mind that odd sizes and shapes can be mixed in with more regular stones to maintain overall consistency, and you can knock off peaks and other formations with a brick chisel and maul, as needed, to make them fit during construction.

- Set Up a Level Line

Use wood stakes and a mason's line to mark the location of the front face of the base of the wall. The string also represents the front of the trench for the wall base. The width (front to back) of the trench should be at least one-half the total wall height. For example, if the wall is 30 inches tall, the trench should be at least 15 inches wide. Place a line level on the string, then pull the string taut from one end, and level the line before tying it off to the stake.

- Excavate the Area

Excavate the area, starting from the string and moving back toward the slope. Dig down 12 inches into the ground to create a flat, level trench for the gravel base and first course of block, which will be below grade. Dig into the slope as needed to create a 6- to 12-inch-wide space between the backside of the wall and the slope, for drainage rock. Measure down from the level line to make sure the excavation is level as you go.

- Add Landscape Fabric

Cover the excavated area with strips of landscape fabric (not plastic) laid perpendicular to the front of the wall and extending a few feet onto the upper-level ground. Overlap adjacent strips of fabric by 6 inches. Cut the strips to length with a utility knife.

- Build the Wall Base

Fill the trench with 5 inches of compactible gravel. Rake the gravel so it is flat and level, then tamp it thoroughly with a hand tamp or a rented power tamper. Add a 1-inch layer of coarse sand over the gravel. Smooth the sand with a short 2x4 board so it is flat and level.

- Lay the First Course

Set large, flat stones along the front edge of the trench to build the first course. Add or remove sand beneath each stone, as needed, so the tops of the stones are flush with one another. Use a 4-foot carpenter's level set across multiple stones to make sure the stones are level as you work.

- Lay the Second Course

Place the next course of stones on top of the first, offsetting (or "staggering") the joints between stones with those in the first course, similar to the 1-over-2 pattern of bricklaying. This adds strength to the wall. Also, set the front faces of the stones about 1/2 inch back (toward the slope) from the front of the first course. This creates a slight stair-step pattern, called batter, that helps the wall resist forces imposed by the slope. As you place each stone, check that there is as little wobble as possible. You can use small, flat rocks as shims to prevent wobbling.

- Begin Back-Filling the Wall

Fill the space between the wall and the slope with drainage gravel. Rake the gravel flat and level, and tamp it thoroughly with the hand tamp. Back-fill only up to the highest course on the wall.

- Install More Courses

Lay the third and subsequent courses of stone, using the same techniques, adding 1/2 inch of batter for each course and staggering the joints with the course below. Starting with the third course, install "deadman" stones long stones that reach back into the slope to help tie the wall into the earth. Place a deadman every 4 feet or so, and dig into the slope, as needed, so the stones sit level front to back. A wall that is 30 inches or less needs only one course with deadmen, but plan on two courses for a taller wall. Back-fill the wall with gravel as you go.

- Complete the Top of the Wall

Fold the landscape fabric over the drainage gravel as you near the top of the wall. You can do this before the last one or two standard courses or before the capstones (the top-most course), depending on how much soil you'd like at the top of the wall (for growing grass). Lay the final course of stones and/or the capstones to complete the top of the wall. If desired, you can glue the capstones to the course below to help keep them in place, using masonry adhesive.

- Back-Fill With Soil

Trim the landscape fabric so it is just below the top of the wall. Cover the landscape fabric and back-fill behind the top of the wall with soil, as desired. To grow grass in this area, the soil layer should be at least 6 inches thick.

Stone Retaining Wall Tips

You can build a stone wall with natural fieldstone that you have on your property, provided the stones are flat enough for stacking. If you have to buy stone, choose a flat stone, such as flagstone, or a cut stone like ashlar. Flat or cut stones are much easier to work with than fieldstone and will make a sturdier wall.

To create a more natural or aged look, plan to add plants in various places in the wall. Rougher stone will automatically have gaps large enough for packing in soil and planting. If you use cut stone, plan for plantable gaps when building the wall.

They don't need to be large and should not compromise the wall's integrity. Cascading plants, such as creeping thyme, perennial yellow alyssum, and annual white alyssum, look very attractive spilling down the sides of stone retaining walls. Herbs also work well growing on or near rock walls.

How to Build a Concrete Patio

A concrete slab patio is hard to beat. It's flat and smooth, so it's suitable for all sorts of furniture and outdoor activities. It's easy to keep clean and doesn't leave grit on your shoes to be tracked into the house (like gravel patios). It's virtually impervious to weeds and does not shift with seasonal changes, unlike paver and stone patios. Perhaps best of all, if you build the patio yourself, concrete is much cheaper than brick, stone, and other hard patio surfaces.

The challenge of building with concrete is, not surprisingly, the concrete itself. Once concrete is mixed, there's no turning back, as it hardens no matter what.

The key to success is preparation: Make sure the forms are well-secured and that all of your tools (and helpers) are ready to work for you. After the concrete is poured and screeded— the initial process of leveling and smoothing the surface, done with a long 2x4 board—it's important to let the concrete set up properly before you start the final finishing. When the finishing begins, don't overwork the concrete. Bringing up too much moisture weakens the finished surface.

You can pour concrete within a fairly wide temperature range, but for beginners it's best to wait for dry, warm weather. Rain can ruin a concrete finish, and freezing temperatures can ruin an entire concrete slab. To slow the curing process in very hot, dry weather, use a shade to keep the concrete out of direct sunlight, and mist the concrete with water as needed to prevent premature curing, which weakens the finished product.

- Codes and Regulations

In most areas, large concrete slabs require approval from the city's building and/or zoning department. Slabs are permanent structures, and as such are subject to zoning restrictions. Local building code rules may dictate several elements of the design, including the thicknesses of the gravel base and the slab, the type of concrete and its internal reinforcement, and the need (or not) for a moisture barrier under the slab. Contact your city's building department for recommendations specific to your project.

Note: Before breaking ground, call 8-1-1, the national "Call Before You Dig" hotline, to have all underground utility lines marked on your property. This is a free service, but it can take a few days, so call well in advance of starting your project.

What You'll Need:

Equipment / Tools

- Tape measure
- Hammer
- Mason's lines
- Line level
- Carpenter's level
- Straight 2x4 board
- Shovel
- Plate compactor
- Steel rake
- Wood saw
- Drill and screwdriver bit
- Concrete mixer
- Wheelbarrow
- Mason's trowel
- Darby

- Concrete groover

- Concrete edger

- Wood float

- Medium-bristle push broom (optional)

- Materials

- Stakes

- Compactible gravel

- 2x4 lumber

- 3 1/2-inch and 2-inch deck screws

- Vegetable oil

- Bagged concrete (or ready-mix)

- Plastic sheeting

- Concrete sealer (optional)

- 1/2-inch x 3 1/2-inch expansion joint strips (as needed)

- Spray adhesive or concrete nails (as needed)

Instructions:

- Set Up the Guide Strings

Set up guide strings to represent the edges of the patio, using stakes and mason's lines. Start by driving two stakes at each corner of the patio area, placing the stakes about 1 foot beyond the edges of the patio. Tie mason's lines between pairs of opposing stakes to create a square or rectangular layout. The points where the strings intersect mark the patio corners. The strings should be at least 6 inches above the ground.

- Square the String Layout

Check the string layout for square by measuring diagonally between opposing corners where the strings intersect. If the two diagonal measurements are equal, the layout is square. If they are not equal, adjust the stake positions as needed until the measurements are equal.

- Slope the Strings

Slope the strings so that the patio will slope away from the house at 1/8 inch per foot. For example, if the patio measures 8 feet from one end to the other, it should slope downward by 1 inch over its length. Measure down 1 inch (in this example) from the strings at the low end of the patio, and mark the stakes, then move the strings to the marks.

- Excavate the Patio Area

Remove all vegetation in the patio area, extending the edges about 6 inches beyond all sides of the patio (to make room for setting the concrete form). Excavate the soil to a depth of 8 inches. As you work, measure down from the layout lines to gauge the excavation depth. It's usually easiest to dig out the sides to full depth, then dig out the interior area, using a long, straight 2x4 and level to make sure the entire area is level (from side to side; it will slope in the other direction). Tamp the soil thoroughly with a rented plate compactor.

- Install the Gravel Base

Fill the excavated area with 2 inches of compactible gravel. Rake the gravel smooth, then compact it thoroughly with the plate compactor. Add 2 more inches of gravel, and rake it smooth. Measure down from the layout strings and use the 2x4 with a carpenter's level on top to make sure the gravel is level side-to-side and slopes end-to-end to follow the strings. Compact the second layer of gravel.

- Build the Concrete Form

Construct a concrete form with 2x4 lumber and 3 1/2-inch screws. The interior dimensions of the form should equal the final dimensions of the concrete slab. Set the form onto the gravel base. Measure the diagonals (as with the string layout) to make sure the form is square.

- Secure the Form

Drive wood stakes all around the outside of the form, spacing them about 2 feet apart. The stakes should extend about 3 1/2 inches above the ground. Lift the form so its top surface is 4 inches above the ground and secure it to the stakes with 2-inch deck screws driven through the stakes and into the form boards. Maintain even spacing between the form and the guide strings. Secure the form at all of the stakes, then remove the guide strings and stakes.

Note: If the patio slab will abut an existing concrete structure, such as a garage slab, driveway, or house foundation, install strips of expansion joint material onto the existing structure, using spray adhesive or concrete nails. Align the top of the expansion joint strip with the tops of the form boards. This expansion joint will isolate the new concrete from the old to help prevent cracking.

- Pour the Concrete

Coat the interior surfaces of the form with vegetable oil so the concrete won't stick to them. Mix fiber-reinforced concrete (or as specified by building code) in a rented concrete mixer, following the manufacturer's directions. Transfer the mixed concrete to a wheelbarrow, then dump the concrete inside the form in piles. Distribute the concrete with a shovel to fill the form. Repeat until the form is filled to the top.

- Screed the Concrete

Use the long, straight 2x4 board to screed the top of the concrete. Rest the board on top of both sides of the form, and move the board back and forth in a sawing motion while pulling it backward. Use a shovel to remove excess concrete, or add concrete to fill in low spots, as needed, so the top of concrete is flat and level. If the slab is larger than 8 feet in either dimension, cut control joints at 8-foot intervals, using the 2x4 and a mason's trowel. Position the board across the form, then follow the edge of the board with the trowel, slicing down into the concrete to separate the gravel inside and create a control joint (to control cracking).

• Finish the Concrete

Let the concrete cure until the "bleed water" (moisture that rises to the surface after screeding) disappears, then smooth the surface with a darby. Allow the bleed water to disappear again. If you made control joints, go over all of the joints with a groover tool, using the 2x4 to ensure straight lines. Round over the edges of the slab with an edger tool. Smooth out any blemishes in the surface with a wood float.

• Add a Broom Finish (Optional)

"Broom" the surface of the concrete, if desired, to add slip-resistance. Drag a push broom backwards across the surface of the concrete in straight, parallel lines. After the entire slab is broomed, you can smooth the edges and control joints again with an edger and trowel or leave the broom lines extending to the edges of the slab.

- Cover and Cure the Patio Slab

Cover the concrete with plastic sheeting. Keep the concrete moist while curing by lifting the plastic and misting the concrete with water each day. Otherwise, keep the concrete covered. Repeat this process for one to two weeks.

- Complete the Job

Remove the plastic from the concrete. Disassemble the wood form, and remove all stakes from the ground. Backfill around the slab with soil or other material. If desired, seal the concrete with concrete sealant, following the manufacturer's directions.

- Tips for Building a Concrete Patio

Buying concrete in dry, premixed bags makes sense for relatively small patio slabs. To get an idea of how many bags you would need, a 50-square-foot slab at 4 inches thick needs about 28 80-pound bags or 38 60-pound bags. You can buy bagged concrete a local home center or lumberyard, and you can rent a concrete mixer at any large rental outlet.

For large slabs, consider ordering ready-mix concrete delivered by a concrete truck. Ready-mix is more expensive than bagged concrete, but it's far more convenient, and you don't have the labor of mixing the concrete or the concern of getting the mix just right. Discuss your plans with local concrete companies to compare costs and to make sure your site is suitable for ready-mix delivery.

How to Make an Easy Brick Patio Pattern for Beginners
Patio bricks can be laid in a variety of different patterns. The pattern is strictly for looks, and the brick surface will perform the same regardless of the pattern. For beginners, it makes sense to use a simple pattern that requires little or no cutting of bricks. Perhaps the best option is the basket weave, which is decorative and eye-catching but also very easy to install. And if you choose to build a square or rectangular patio and size it to fit the bricks, you shouldn't have to cut any bricks at all.

The best bricks to use for this project are paving bricks or brick pavers. These are about 2 inches thick and have smooth, solid faces to create a nice walking surface. For a basket weave design, which has a checkerboard pattern, you want the widths of two bricks to equal the length of one. Therefore, an ideal size of paver is 4 inches wide by 8 inches long.

The easiest way to install a brick paver patio is the sandset method. The bricks are laid on the ground, over a layer of compacted gravel topped by landscape fabric and a smooth layer of sand. After the bricks are laid, you sweep sand into the cracks between the pavers to lock them in place.

Why We Use Paving Bricks

- Codes and Regulations

Call your city office to learn about all building code requirements, zoning laws, or land use restrictions that may apply to your project. In most areas, you do not need a building permit for a simple paver patio, but zoning and land use rules may come into play. If the proposed patio is located near a property line or an easement or right of way, the city may require a survey of the property and possibly other documentation before you can build.

Note: If clay bricks are kiln-fired, they are harder than concrete.

What You'll Need:

Equipment / Tools

- Tape measure
- 8 Stakes
- Small sledgehammer
- Mason's line
- Line level
- Shovel
- Rake
- Long, straight 2x4 board
- Carpenter's level
- Hand tamp or plate compactor
- Rubber mallet
- Plywood scrap
- Broom
- Garden hose
- Materials

- Paving bricks

- Brick patio edging

- Compactible gravel

- Landscape fabric

- Sand

Instructions:

- Mark the Patio Edges

Use stakes and mason's line to create layout lines for the patio. Base the dimensions on the brick paver size; the lines should represent the outer edges of the brick, not the edging. You can create a layout with just four stakes, but a better method is to drive two stakes at each corner, placed about 2 feet beyond the sides of the patio. When you tie lines to the stakes, the points where the lines cross mark the actual corners of the patio. This setup allows you to excavate and prepare the entire patio area without having the stakes get in the way.

Make sure the string layout is square by measuring diagonally between opposing corners (where the strings meet); the layout is square when the diagonal measurements are equal.

- Slope the Strings

Place a line level on each layout string and adjust one end of the string up or down, as needed, so the line is perfectly level. Then, lower the strings on the downhill end of the patio 1/4 inch per linear foot of patio length. For example, if the patio is 10 feet long, it will slope down 2 1/2 inches from one end to the other. The downhill end is where you want water to run off of the patio; typically, this should be the end farthest from the house so surface water sheds away from the house foundation.

- Excavate the Area

Excavate the patio area to a depth of 8 inches, extending the excavation about 6 inches beyond the brick layout on all sides. Slope the soil to follow the layout lines, measuring down from the lines as you go to maintain an 8-inch depth. Excavate to full depth along the two sides, then dig out the center, checking with a long, straight 2x4 board and a level to ensure the entire area is flat and level from side to side; the soil base will slope toward the downhill end but will be level from side to side. Tamp the soil thoroughly with a hand tamp or a rented plate compactor.

- Add a Gravel Base

Pour compactible gravel inside the excavated area to a depth of 4 inches. Rake the gravel smooth and level, slope it to follow the string layout, and tamp it so it is thoroughly compacted.

- Install Paver Edging

Install paver edging along the perimeter of the patio, following the manufacturer's directions. Standard plastic edging is designed for brick patios and is largely concealed when the bricks are in place. It is installed with metal spikes. Line up bricks along the edges to make sure the edging placement is accurate (so that you won't have to cut any bricks). The edging should fit snugly against the test-fit bricks. Remove the test-fit bricks, keeping the edging in place.

- Add the Sand Layer

Lay landscape fabric over the gravel; this suppresses weeds and separates the gravel from the sand layer. Pour 2 inches of sand over the landscape fabric. Use the 2x4 as a screed to smooth and level the sand. There should be 2 inches between the top of the sand and the top of the patio edging. Remove the layout strings and stakes.

Note : Spray the sand with a gentle mist of water until it is thoroughly soaked. This helps to concentrate and compact the sand.

- Lay the First Row of Bricks

Lay the first bricks, starting in one corner and running along the edging to complete a row. Alternate each pair of bricks so that two are horizontal, then two are vertical, and so on. Press the bricks gently into the sand, and put them together as closely as possible. Tap the bricks with a rubber mallet to settle them into the sand, if necessary.

Run a mason's line across the first row, aligned with the leading edges of the bricks. Pull the line taut and secure it at the ends with stakes, or simply clamp them to the edging. Straighten the bricks in the first row, as needed, so all leading edges are even with the line.

- Lay the Remaining Bricks

Install the remaining bricks, one row at a time, moving the mason's line for each row. For comfort and to prevent moving the installed bricks, lay a sheet of plywood atop the bricks to kneel on while you work. The last row should fit snugly against the edging.

- Lock the Bricks With Sand

Spread sand over the bricks, then sweep across the patio surface with a push broom to work the sand into the cracks. Sweep in multiple directions to reach all cracks, adding sand as you go until the cracks are filled. Gently spray the patio with a garden hose to settle the sand in the cracks. Spread and sweep more sand into the cracks, and spray again, until the cracks are completely filled and the sand is settled.

- Backfill the Edging

Backfill behind the brick edging with soil and sod or other landscape material. This partially hides the edging to create a finished look, and it helps to hold the pavers and edging in place.

Tips for Building a Brick Patio :

If you need to cut some bricks to fit your layout, you can use a hammer and masonry chisel or a circular saw with a masonry blade. But if you have a lot of cuts to make, it's worth it to rent a brick splitter or a masonry wet saw for half a day. These tools make much faster, cleaner cuts than a hammer or handheld saw. The best blade to use for saw cuts is a diamond blade. Alternatively, you can use an abrasive blade, but it may wear down quickly and won't cut as cleanly.

How to Lay a Flagstone Patio

Flagstone path leading to patio bordered by perennials including cow parsley (Anthriscus sylvestris) 'Ravenswing', cranesbill (Geranium) and columbines (Aquilegia), Wall, Lummi Island, WA, USA

Laying flagstone patios in stone dust or sand, as opposed to mortar or concrete, is known as dry-set or sand-set. Dry construction is much easier for do-it-yourselfers because you can build directly on the ground, while mortared stone requires a concrete slab foundation to prevent cracking in the mortar. For a lasting installation, a dry-set stone patio does need a foundation, though. It's best to start with several inches of compacted gravel, followed by a layer of stone dust, also called decomposed granite, or DG.

The DG is pulverized stone and contains small pieces along with gravel-size and sand-size particles. The variation in particle sizes allows the material to compact well. And while it is still loose, you can use it to level the stones, just as you would with sand. You can buy flagstone and DG at local stone yards and landscaping materials suppliers.

When choosing stone for the project, select the largest stones you can maneuver by hand, and choose them for consistent thickness and appearance. The stones should be at least 1 1/2 inches thick for strength; 2 inches thick is better. Note that "flagstone" merely describes the stones' wide, flat shape; flagstone comes in many different types of stone.

- Codes and Regulations

Check with your city's building department to learn about rules and requirements that may pertain to your project. Chances are, you won't need a building permit for this project, but you may need to gain approval from the zoning department, which governs land use.

Most important, call 8-1-1, the national "Call Before You Dig" hotline, to have all underground utility lines marked on your property. You must do this before breaking ground. The service is free but can take several days, so call well in advance of starting your project.

What You'll Need :

Equipment / Tools

- Tape measure
- 8 Stakes
- Small sledgehammer
- Mason's line
- Line level
- Shovel
- Rake
- Carpenter's level

- Hand tamp or plate compactor

- Broom

- Garden hose

- Materials

- Compactible gravel

- Decomposed granite (stone dust)

- Flagstone

- Fill material (as desired)

- Long, straight 2x4 board

Instructions :

- Mark the Patio Edges

Set up mason's lines to represent the perimeter of the patio. Drive two stakes at each corner, about 2 feet beyond the sides of the patio perimeter. Tie a mason's line to opposing pairs of stakes to create a square or rectangular layout (use a square layout if the patio will be circular). You will have a total of four strings; the points where the strings intersect represent the corners of the patio area. This layout method allows you to excavate and prepare the entire patio area without having to move the stakes.

- Square up the Layout

Confirm that the string layout is square by measuring diagonally between opposing corners (where the strings meet); the layout is square when the diagonal measurements are equal. Adjust the positions of the stakes, as needed, to square the layout.

- Slope the Layout Strings

Level and slope the strings based on the position of the patio: The patio surface should be level from side to side (typically parallel to the house) and should slope down and away from the house from end to end at a rate of about 2 inches per 10 linear feet. For example, if the patio is 10 feet long, it will be 2 inches higher at the house end than at the opposite end. This ensures that surface water drains away from the house (or other structures).

To level and slope the strings, place a line level on each layout string and adjust one end of the string up or down, as needed, so the line is perfectly level, then tie off the string. Keep in mind that all of the strings should be at the same height. Then, readjust the two strings running down the sides of the patio to set the correct slope. For a 10-foot-long patio, lower the strings 2 inches on the stakes at the lower end of the patio. Finally, adjust the perpendicular string on the lower end of the patio so it is even with ends of the sloped strings.

- Excavate the Patio Area

Remove all grass and other vegetation in the patio area (defined by the strings), then excavate the soil to a depth of 6 inches plus the thickness of the flagstone. For example, if the flagstone is 2 inches thick, excavate a total of 8 inches. This is to make the patio flush with the surrounding ground; you can dig less deep if you want the stones to lie higher than the ground.

Measure down from the strings to gauge the excavation depth. It's usually easiest to dig to full depth right under the strings, then clear out the soil in between, checking with a long, straight 2x4 and a level to make sure the ground is level from side to side (it won't be level from end to end because of the slope). Tamp the soil with a hand tamp or a rented plate compactor.

Note: Don't kill the grass. Move your piles of excavated turf and soil off of your grass within two days so you don't over-stress it.

- Install the Gravel Base

Add a two-inch layer of compactible gravel over the patio area. Rake the gravel smooth and level, then tamp it thoroughly. Add two more inches, then smooth and tamp. As with the excavation, measure down from the strings to gauge the thickness of the gravel and to maintain the proper slope.

- Add the DG Layer

Add a 2-inch layer of decomposed granite over the gravel base. Rake the DG smooth, and level it side-to-side with the long board and level. Tamp the layer thoroughly. Remove the stakes and mason's lines.

- Organize the Stones

Stack or lay out the stones you will use for the patio surface on a broad, flat area, such as the surrounding grass or a driveway. Arrange the pieces by size and shape so you can select them readily as you lay them into the patio.

- Lay the Patio Stones

Place the stones onto the DG surface, starting at one end and working toward the other. Place the stones as close together as desired. You will fill the gaps later with sand, gravel, or even soil and grass or other plants. Vary the size, shape, and coloring of stones for a random pattern, which looks most natural.

- Level the Stones

Level each stone, as needed, by adding or removing DG underneath the stone. Each stone should be stable and at the same height as the surrounding stones. Stone edges that stick up create tripping hazards.

- Fill the Gaps

Fill the gaps between stones with sand, DG, or gravel. Sweep the material across the patio with a broom to push it in to the cracks. Spray the patio with a garden hose to settle the fill material, then sweep more filler across the stones to fill the gaps as desired. Alternatively, you can fill the gaps with a potting soil mix and plant grass or traffic-tolerant ground cover plants between stones.

Flagstone Patio Tips :

Some of the stones in your dry-set patio inevitably will move over time, due to use and to seasonal freeze-thaw cycles. But fixing shifted stones is easy. Simply dig out the sand, gravel, or soil around a problem stone, then pry up the stone using your hands or a flat pry bar. If the stone is too high, remove some bed material from under the stone; if the stone is too low, add some bed material. Reposition the stone and make sure it's flush with the surrounding stones, then repack the joints around the stone.

How to Build a Stone Sidewalk or Garden Path

A stone walkway has rustic charm that is ideal for a cottage garden design but is equally suitable for any natural landscape plan. (By contrast, a brick path is better suited to formal landscaping.) While stone paths sometimes are laid in mortar, this requires a concrete foundation and experience with stone masonry. A simple sandset path is much easier and is perfect for DIY installation. With this technique, the stones are simply laid onto a bed of sand, which keeps the stones stable and makes it easy to get everything level. When you're done, you can fill the spaces between the stones with sand or gravel or even plants that can tolerate foot traffic.

Choosing stone for a walkway is mostly a matter of taste, as any wide, flat stones will do. Most walkways are made with flagstone, which describes a shape of stone rather than a specific type of rock. It's usually best to choose a type that is locally available, as this keeps the cost down, both for the rock and the delivery. Make sure any stone you use has a natural surface and is thick enough to be strong (don't use polished stone, which is very slippery when wet). Most flagstone that is 2 to 3 inches thick is ideal. Thicker stones are stronger and heavier than thinner pieces; they're also often less expensive, due to their weight.

What You'll Need :

Equipment / Tools

- Stakes and string or 2 garden hoses

- Flat spade

- Shovel

- Wheelbarrow

- Hand tamp

- Small sledgehammer (as needed for edging)

- Utility knife

- Scrap 2x4 board

- Carpenter's level

- Materials

- Edging material (optional)

- Landscape fabric and staples

- Sand

- Large, flat stones

- Gravel, potting mix, plants (optional)

Instructions:

- Lay Out the Walkway

Mark the path of your walkway, using stakes and string (for a straight path) or two garden hoses (for a curving path). If the walkway will be used for frequent traffic, such as a path between a driveway and a front door, make sure it is wide enough for two people to pass by each other comfortably. Small garden paths or those leading to secret nooks in the landscape can be sized for a single person. Set up strings or hoses on both sides of the path.

- Excavate the Path

Use a flat spade or sod cutter to slice through grass along the path's edges, following the strings or garden hoses. Remove all grass or other vegetation (including all roots) in the path area. Dig out the soil to a depth of 5 inches (for 3-inch-thick stone), creating a flat, smooth base. Tamp the soil firmly with a hand tamp or simply by walking repeatedly over the ground.

- Install Edging (optional)

Install edging material along both sides of the path, if desired, following the manufacturer's directions. You can use many different types of edging, such as galvanized metal, plastic brick paver edging, or pressure-treated wood timbers. If you don't use edging, the edge of grass or soil along the path will help keep the stones in place.

- Apply Landscape Fabric

Lay landscape fabric over the soil along the entire path. Try to use a continuous piece as much as possible. If you must use multiple pieces, overlap their edges by at least 12 inches. Trim the fabric along the sides of the path with a utility knife, and secure the fabric to the soil with landscape fabric staples.

- Add a Sand Layer

Add two inches of sand over the landscape fabric. Smooth the sand so it is flat and level, using a 2x4 board that is slightly smaller than the width of the path.

Note: Spray the sand with water to help concentrate and compact it prior to setting the stones.

- Lay Out the Stones

Lay out the path stones to one side of the walkway so all of them are visible. The idea is to see the size and shape of each stone so you can pick and choose the best fit as you lay the walkway.

- Install the Stones

Begin placing stones into the sand bed of the walkway, fitting them together as desired. Leave small gaps between stones if you will fill the gaps with sand or gravel; leave wider gaps (about 2 inches) if you will plant between the rocks. Set each stone so it is stable (without rocking) and is level with the surrounding stones.

Use a carpenter's level to check each stone for level and to level across to other stones as you work. Add or remove sand beneath each stone to raise or lower it, as needed. Alternate large and small stones as well as different shapes and colors for a natural, random look.

Laying Marble Plates :

- Fill the Gaps

Add sand or gravel to fill the gaps between the stones, as desired. Spread the sand with a broom, spray the walkway with water to settle the sand, then fill the gaps again, repeating until they are full. If you're planting the walkway, fill the gaps with a potting soil mix, then add "stepable" plants, such as wooly thyme, sedum, or bugleweed.

Note:

If the area where you will install the sidewalk is very wet or is prone to flooding during heavy rains, consider adding a 4- to 6-inch bed of compactible gravel under the landscaping fabric and sand layer. Gravel provides a more stable base than soil, and it drains readily to help prevent pooling. You might also set the height of the path a few inches higher than the surrounding ground to help keep the path drier.

If you use large stones, which may collect water, slope the stones to one side of the path so water sheds from their surfaces. Make sure to slope away from the house or other structures. You can create a slope with the entire sand bed, if desired, but it's usually easier to slope each stone as you go, using a level. They should slope at about 1/8 inch per foot. For example, if a stone is 2 feet wide, it should be 1/4 inch lower on one side than the other.

Types of Wooden Fences

- Zig-zag style wooden fence in a grassland environment

When it is time to select fencing for your property, you may be overwhelmed by how many types of wooden fences and other options there are from which to choose, but the decision largely comes down to two considerations:

- Form (stylistic considerations)
- Function (what practical purpose the fencing will serve)

Sometimes, there is a happy marriage between form and function, but such is not always the case. For instance, chain-link fencing and other metal products often make for superior security fences. Therefore, if the intended function of your fencing is security, you may have to choose between form and function: the style of your house may cry out for a wooden fence, but security concerns may convince you to go with the metal.

Form (stylistic considerations)

In choosing between types of wooden fences, consider their potential for compatibility both with your house style and with your landscape-design style:

Split-rail wood fences and other wood fence designs marked by rough and rugged posts and rails have long been a favorite with:

- Ranch-style houses
- Landscape designs with a Southwestern theme (U.S.)
- Picket-style fencing seems a natural fit for:
- Cottage-style homes
- Landscape designs inspired by English cottage gardens

Function (what practical purpose the fencing will serve)
There are special circumstances in which wooden fences, despite their beauty, may not be your best choice for fencing. Sometimes, for example, a homeowner in the market for fencing needs to keep animals in the yard dogs, for instance. In this case, electric dog fences may be the answer. There are also times when the issue is keeping animals out of the yard deer, for instance. Various types of deer fencing serve this function.

Security is another practical function many homeowners demand from fencing, a function for which metal fencing is considered superior to wooden fences.

Wooden fences are an excellent choice for privacy fencing, though, whether it be in terms of noise barriers or visual barriers. Along with their vinyl copy-cats, they provide some of the most attractive fencing options available when your chief concern is creating a backyard sanctuary.

The stockade style offers an example of a wood fence design that can afford a solid visual barrier between your yard and your neighbor's, resulting in almost total privacy. While masonry work such as brick can do the same, it costs significantly more than does a wooden fence.

Others prefer a compromise on privacy, choosing styles with a certain amount of airiness to them, to avoid fencing out the outer world altogether. Tall picket fencing, for example, can afford partial privacy, as can lattice fencing. Another variation on this compromise is to create a privacy screen using shrubs instead of fencing.

One factor in choosing between the different types of wooden fences is their potential for compatibility with one's landscape design. Solid wooden fences can provide compelling backdrops for plantings, while the airier designs can serve either as foregrounds or backgrounds for flower borders. Ideally, your fencing will work in harmony with other landscaping elements to create compelling visual interest in your landscape design.

How to Build A Deck

Building your own deck is a tempting DIY project that many people complete successfully, and others regret ever attempting. Entire books have been written on the subject, and it's not something that should be attempted if you're unsure of your basic carpentry skills. This article will give you an overview of the process, focusing on the basic principles of construction, but detailed plans and other information that's required for actual construction.

- Codes, Permits, and Planning

Before even contemplating a deck, check with your local building authorities to determine if there are any restrictions and if building permits are required. Many communities have set-back rules that determine how close you can build to property lines, as well as requirements for heights, structural supports, and dimensions for railings and stairways.

Your building inspection office really should be the first place you go, as they can tell you much about how you should build, whether you can build, and variations in deck construction all of which will tell you if you want to build at all. Did you know, for example, that decks must be supported by footings that reach below the winter frost line in your region? This will mean you might have to dig holes and pour fittings that are four feet deep or even more if you live in a cold region.

Be aware that building a deck (any deck) will have you doing a fair amount of problem-solving. The more carefully you consider all your options and possibilities up front, the smoother your work will go. For example, will your deck be anchored to your house , a construction style that requires that you remove siding--or might it be possible to make your deck freestanding to avoid this complication? This and many other possibilities should be considered up front to make for a smooth project.

Do your homework. Obtain a good blueprint plan for your deck, or read a couple of good books on the subject. Make hand sketches of the deck you plan to build, and walk through the steps mentally before starting the more time spent visualizing the work that's about to come, the better.

You Will Need:

Tools and Materials

Deck building is a full-featured construction project, and you may need to buy or borrow quite a few tools if you don't already own them. And the list of materials is impressive as well. Be aware that even a simple deck can cost you several thousand dollars in lumber, hardware and possibly new tools.

Here are typical tools required to build a deck:

- Circular saw
- Table saw
- Power miter saw
- Shovel and post-hole digger
- Cement mixer or wheelbarrow
- Carpenter's level
- Carpenter's square
- Caulk gun
- Drill and bits
- Wrenches
- Hammer
- Tape measure
- Eye protection
- Particle respiration mask

As for materials, you may need:

- Metal flashing
- Caulk
- Pre-mixed concrete mix
- Gravel or crushed stone
- Cinder blocks
- Post caps
- Post bases
- Seismic ties
- Joist hangers
- Cardboard tube concrete forms
- Metal Rebar
- HDG bolts or lag screws, and washers
- Joist hanger nails
- Deck screws or stainless steel or HDG nails

Instructions:

As regards the lumber, there are too many variables involved to give precise dimensions or quantities. Suffice it to say you will need a lot of it, and in a lot of different dimensions, including 6 x 6 or 4 x 4 posts, 2 x 10 or 2 x 12s for joists and beams, 2 x 4s for other structural members, and 1x dimension lumber or decking boards for the surface of your deck. Again, your local residential building codes will dictate the size of lumber you will need for the various structural components of your deck.

While interior carpentry projects can be framed with ordinary pine lumber, outdoor projects like a deck require lumber suited for exposure to moisture. This means that you will use wood species like cedar or redwood for some key components, and pressure-treated pine for many of the key structural members.

Basic Construction Variation of a Deck

Decks that rest smack up against a house are usually anchored to the house with bolts (or lag screws). This must be done by attachment to solid wood, usually the rim joist or studs underlying the house siding. For the non-carpenter, removing your house's siding is a pretty scary proposition. There is, however, an alternative method: the freestanding deck. Freestanding decks are a bit more work because the house-end of the freestanding deck will have to rest on additional post footings rather than being connected to the house. That means extra digging for you and additional concrete work. But for the sake of your peace of mind, this alternative may be worth the extra work. Another advantage is that in some communities, a structure that is not directly attached to the house does not need a building permit for construction.

Instructions:

- Preparing the Site

Assuming you have found or created your deck design plans and assembled the necessary tools and supplies, the first stage of actual physical work will come in preparing the site.

Using stakes and string, outline the shape of the deck on the building site. If your deck is a simple square or rectangle, measure diagonally from corner to corner, both ways; a square layout will have diagonals with the same measurements.

Using a shovel, remove any grass or weeds from this measured area to form your working space. Later, before closing off this working space with decking, you can apply mulch over this space to suppress weeds. But for now, your main concern is to furnish yourself with as level a working space as possible. This will be important later in the project when you dig holes for footings or concrete piers that will need to be installed perfectly level.

Carefully mark out where the ledger board will attach to your house. This ledger will support and anchor the side of the deck that is adjacent to the house. The level at which the top of the header board rests should be the same as the level of your joists, which will form the framework upon which the surface decking will lie. It is critical to ensure that the header is not only at the proper height but also that it is level. Consult your deck plans when outlining the position of the ledger board on the house.

Now mark out the location for the footing posts on the building site. How many supports you will need, and how deep footings will need to be, are dictated both by your building plans and the requirements of your building inspection office.

- Install the Ledger

The ledger board, usually a 2 x 10 or 2 x 12 board will be anchored directly to your house framing and will form the structural side of the deck against your house. The general procedure goes like this: Remove the siding where the header board must go. Tuck flashing up under the piece of siding that remains above this area. Extend the flashing down the side of the house, low enough that it will extend below the bottom of the ledger board once it is installed. This flashing will prevent water from getting behind the framing.

The ledger board is then attached over the metal flashing with bolts or lag screws. Make sure to seal behind the ledger with caulk to further ensure no moisture can enter.

- Install the Footings and Posts

Now you will install the vertical posts that will support the beams, which will, in turn, provide the main support for the beam.

Dig holes to whatever depth is dictated by your building inspection office, then pour concrete and install 6 x 6 or 4 x 4 posts to the required height. Posts can be embedded into the concrete itself, but a better method is to use cardboard tube forms, then embed metal post anchors in the wet concrete at the top of the form. The wooden posts are then attached to these anchors after the concrete dries.

Whatever method used, it is critical that the posts be exactly plumb, and that they are cut off at precisely the right height as dictated by your building plans. Many builders find it easiest to install the posts first, then cut them all off to the desired height.

- Install Support Beams

In most deck construction plans, one or more horizontal beams are now installed. These beams will provide support for the joists soon to follow. Generally, the deck joists will be attached on one end to the ledger board with joist hangers and will rest on the other end by a beam that's supported by the posts you have just installed.

There are many different configurations for posts and beams, so carefully follow your deck plans at this point. A very common method is for beams to be constructed from a pair of 2 x 10s sandwiched together and rested on top of the posts, where they are held in place by metal beam saddles.

In some deck plans, the beam will be set some distance inside the outside edge of the deck, so that the deck hangs extends the beam in cantilever fashion. In other deck plans, the beam itself may form the outside edge of the deck, forming an anchoring surface to which the joists can be attached.

 A very large deck may require two or even more beams to support the heavy load, while small decks require only one small support beam.

- Install the Joists

Now you will install the principle framework of the deck, which includes interior joists spaced every 12 or 16" apart, as well as rim joists, which form the outside edge of the deck. One end of each joist will be attached to the ledger board with metal joist hangers, while the other end will either rest on top of the support beam, or, in some designs will be anchored to the inside face of the beam.

Note that all metal connectors and fasteners must be made with corrosion-resistant fasteners and metal connectors. Ordinary galvanized fasteners are not appropriate if you are using pressure-treated lumber, as the chemicals in the wood can corrode them. Make sure to buy screws, nails and other hardware designed to withstand the chemicals.

Here, too, the spacing of joists and the lumber dimension will be determined both by your deck plans and the requirements of your building inspection office. Very small decks may call for joists built from 2 x 6 lumber, while large decks may require 2 x 10 or 2 x 12 lumber. Load calculations are very complicated, so make sure to consult your building inspection office on requirements for posts, beams, and joists.

- Lay the Decking

Now your deck is beginning to take shape and look like the project you envisioned. The next step is to attach decking boards, which will often be 1x 4 or 1 x 6 lumber, or fabricated decking boards with rounded edges. Another option here will be synthetic decking boards, which are notable for their long life. It is quite common to build the deck structure with pressure-treated lumber, then use synthetic decking materials for the visible decking surface and railings.

Note: depending on the height and style of your deck, you may choose to install stairways and railings prior to laying the surface decking.

Traditionally, decking boards are anchored to the joists with a pair of screws or nails driven into each joist. However, there are also a variety of "blind nailing" or bracket systems now available that allow you to attach decking boards without violating the face of the boards with screws or nails. Whatever method you choose, make sure to leave a uniform gap between decking boards. This ensures that debris will not get trapped between boards.

- Final Steps

For many decks, building stairways and railings will be the next step. Many decks other than ground-hugging platform decks will be required by building codes to have stairways and railings. Stairway construction can be quite complicated, especially if a deck is a high one, where a stairway may even need to have a landing part way down. The main deck railings can also involve a complicated system of posts, rails, and balusters, but they also offer an opportunity for style variation.

You may now be inclined to finish your deck with stain and sealer or paint immediately, but it is often recommended that you wait for a few weeks for this final step, until the lumber in your deck dries out a bit. You should finish your deck before winter sets in, but allowing the deck wood to age slightly will help it absorb the stain and finish better.

What Is a Pergola?

A pergola is an outdoor structure consisting of columns that support a roofing grid of beams and rafters. This roofing grid may be left open or covered so as to create an area sheltered from the elements. Pergolas may be freestanding or attached to a house.

In order to gain a better grasp of the definition for "pergola," it is helpful to compare and contrast it with other outdoor structures with which it is sometimes associated, including:

- Arbors
- Gazebos
- Trellises
- Lattice (or "latticework")
- Carports

An arbor is a landscaping structure very similar to a pergola, but there are differences between the two. If we look at the subtleties, the following distinction can be drawn:

Garden arbors:

- Are relatively simple structures, lacking architectural flourishes such as masonry columns.
- Are relatively small structures.
- Frequently bear curved arches at the top.
- Are increasingly being made from vinyl, rather than more traditional materials.
- Are freestanding (that is, they are not attached to houses, although they may be attached to a fence, in which case they sometimes house a gate).

Pergolas, by contrast, are typically larger structures, often in every dimension (height, width, and length). Sometimes given greater architectural treatment, they may exhibit masonry columns, for instance. Their tops are more often flat.

Traditional pergola design harks back to grand masonry pergolas of the Italian Renaissance. But the term, "pergola" is used more loosely now, and includes wooden structures (as in the photo). Pergolas are often attached to houses, such that they form an outdoor living space that essentially serves as an extension of a home's indoor rooms.

A related outdoor wooden structure is the gazebo. But gazebos always have a closed roof, which is not true of pergolas. Many (but not all) gazebos are further distinguished from pergolas by having:

- A raised floor
- A rounded shape

A "carport" is a structure defined more by its purpose than by how it is made. Carports are used to shelter one's automobile at home in lieu of the more expensive option: a garage. The basic carport is a roof supported by posts. But we have seen more elaborate carports that are essentially pergolas co-opted for car storage.

Pergolas, arbors, trellises, and latticework have all been traditionally used to support vines. A trellis is a portable framework meant to support such plants as vines and climbing rose bushes. It can be made of wood, metal, or vinyl.

Note:

There is overlap between the words, "trellis" and "lattice," but the design of the latter is more specifically associated with a crisscross pattern or a checkerboard pattern. Latticework is often tacked to the sides of an arbor or pergola to give vines something to climb up.

Vines can form a canopy over a pergola, affording shade in summer. Select a large, vigorous vine for this purpose, such as:

- Dutchman's pipe
- Virginia creeper
- Hardy kiwi
- Climbing hydrangea
- Wisteria
- Bougainvillea

But to afford complete shade, plus protection from rain, some people cover their pergolas. One sometimes sees fiberglass used as a covering, but the more upscale homeowners may be interested in retractable shade canopies.

Conclusion

Installing hardscaping can be very hard work. Even under the best climate conditions, these projects can be downright grueling. That is why most homeowners choose to get these jobs done during favorable weather in spring or fall, or during moderate times of summer.

Some hardscape projects are too physically demanding to complete with manual labor alone, and some require heavy equipment. Before you give up on a project because you can't afford the heavy equipment required, look into the option of rentals. Rental stores can be lifesavers for do-it-yourselfers.

Using a rental rather than owning your own heavy equipment is often a prudent option for the homeowner.

www.ingramcontent.com/pod-product-compliance
Lightning Source LLC
Chambersburg PA
CBHW051349150726
48000CB00003B/1105